A Painful History of Medicine

Pox, Pus & Plague
a history of disease
and infection

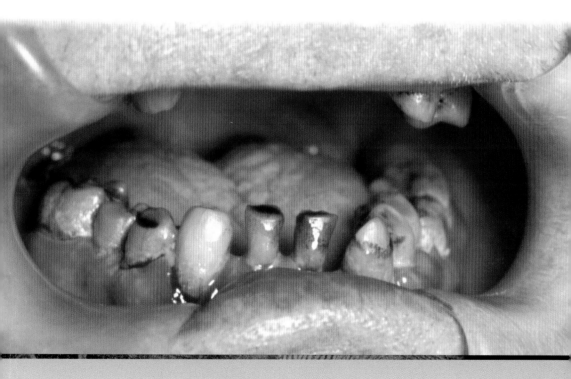

John Townsend

Chicago, Illinois

For information, address the publisher:
Raintree, 100 N. LaSalle, Suite 1200
Chicago, IL 60602
Customer Service: 888-363-4266
Visit our website at www.raintreelibrary.com

Printed and bound in China by South China
Printing Company
09 08 07 06 05
10 9 8 7 6 5 4 3 2 1

Library of Congess Cataloging-inPublication

Townsend, John, 1955-
   Disease : pox, pus & plague / John Townsend.
      p. cm. -- (A painful history of medicine)
   Includes bibliographical references and index.
   ISBN 1-4109-1333-3 (library bdg.-hardcover) --
ISBN 1-4109-1338-4 (pbk.)
   1. Medicine--History--Juvenile literature.
   2. Diseases--History--Juvenile literature.
   3. Epidemiology--History--Juvenile literature.
   I. Title. II. Series: Townsend, John, 1955-
Painful history of medicine.
   R133.5.T69 2005
   616'.009--dc22
   2004014249

Acknowledgments

Alamy Images pp. **16** (Medical on Line), **50–51**
(image100); Art Directors and Trip pp. **7**, **13**, **21**
(Helene Rogers); Bridgeman Art Library pp. **14**
(Alinari Osterreichische Nationalbibliothek,
Vienna, Austria), **16–17** (Guildhall Library,
Corporation of London, UK), **19**, **22** (Private
Collection), **36** (Archives Charmet); (Chicago
Department of Water Management) pp. **24–25**;
Corbis pp. **6** (Lester V Bergman), **8** (Historical
Picture Archive), **11** (Mark Peterson), **12**
(Bettmann), **23** (Hulton-Deutsch Collection), **24**,
26–27, **30–31** (Bettmann), **32** (CDC/PHIL), **35**
(Hulton-Deutsch Collection), **39** (Bettman),
42–43 (Phil Schermeister), **43** (Gideon Mandel),
47 (Children's Hospital & Medical Center),
48–49 (Reuters), **49** (Alan Hindle), **53**; Frank
Graham p. **9**; GettyImages/ PhotoDisc pp. **50**,
51; Hulton Archive pp. **38–39**; Kobal Collection
pp. **36–37**; Mary Evans Picture Library p. **28**;
Medical on Line pp. **10**, **19**, **20**, **29**, **33**, **34–35**,
40–41; Science Photo Library pp. **4–5**
(Custom Medical Stock Photo), **10–11** (Mauro
Fermariello), **14–15** (St Mary's Hospital Medical
School), **18** (John Walsh), **22–23** (Dr Klaus
Boller), **34** (Custom Medical Stock Photo), **41**
(St Mary's Hospital Medical School), **44** (R
Umesh Chandran), **44–45** (Andrew Syred), **45**
(Volker Steger), **46** (Colin Cuthbert); Wellcome
Library, London pp. **27**, **28**, **30**, **32–33**.

Cover photograph of woman in iron lung
reproduced with permission of Corbis/Bettmann.

The author and publisher would like to thank
Dr. Justin Miller, D.O. for his assistance in the
preparation of this book.

Every effort has been made to contact copyright
holders of any material reproduced in this book.
Any omissions will be rectified in subsequent
printings if notice is given to the publishers.

The paper used to print this book comes from
sustainable resources.

Contents

Any words appearing in the text in bold,
like this, are explained in the glossary.
You can also look out for them in the "Word
Bank" at the bottom of each page.

Under Attack

Our bodies do strange things. When they work well, we do not think about them much. When something goes wrong, we soon know. It is amazing that our bodies do not have problems more often. After all, they are always under attack. Our bodies are fighting disease all the time.

From the common cold to nasty **infections** that give us oozing **boils** or rotting flesh, diseases are bad news. Today, we know how to fight some of them. We have had to learn through centuries of pain, **pus, pox, plagues,** and pimples!

Some rashes can spread fast if they are not treated.

Word Bank   **boil**   swollen infection on the skin that is red and sore

Why?

Doctors throughout history have wondered about disease and why some spread so fast.

Two big questions doctors once asked were:
1. *How do people catch diseases?*
2. *How can they be cured?*

Fast facts

We now know many diseases are spread by:
- **Bacteria**: tiny living things that enter the body through the mouth, lungs, or by touch.
- **Viruses**: tiny living things that break into the body's **cells.**

Find out later . . .

*Which disease causes black **vomit**?*

*What is **leprosy**?*

What diseases do people fear today?

organism   living cell or group of cells
pox   any disease that causes a rash of pus-filled sores

Many diseases are caught from other people. Ten thousand years ago, humans first began to live together in large groups, or **tribes.** Diseases could then spread easily from one person to another.

Spreading disease

Sometimes people caught diseases from their animals. Animal food and **dung** attracted insects and rats, which spread more disease. Then, when tribes moved to new areas, they passed their diseases on to other tribes.

Coughs and sneezes

One sneeze can contain millions of **viruses.** They can shoot out of your mouth at up to 100 miles (160 kilometers) per hour. If someone is nearby, he or she will get them all! Ancient people had no idea how deadly their sneezes could be.

Coughs and sneezes spread diseases!

Word Bank   **bowel**   part of the intestine where waste is held before being let out of the body

Egyptians

The ancient Egyptians believed some diseases were caused by blockages in the body. To "unblock" themselves, they tried to **vomit** or open the **bowels** by eating **senna**. They also cut themselves to "bleed away" the disease. Egyptian writings from 3,500 years ago told how to treat a sick person:

> If he is sick in his arm, then make him vomit by feeding him fish and beer. Cover his fingers with watermelon until he is healed. If he is sick in the bowel, the blockage must be cleared.

Viruses

The Egyptians were right to think that blood could carry disease. Over 1,000 viruses can live in one red (oxygen-carrying) blood **cell**. There are five million red blood cells in one drop of blood!

Marks on the face of a 3,000-year-old Egyptian mummy are likely to have been left by the **smallpox** disease.

tribe group of people living closely together, sharing the same beliefs and customs

For centuries, doctors •••• let blood leak out of veins because they thought it was good for the patient.

Greeks

Over 2,000 years ago, the Greeks and the Romans had their share of **plagues.** These deadly diseases spread quickly across large areas. About 2,400 years ago, a plague killed a third of the people living in Athens, Greece.

The Greeks saw how weather, soil, and water affected people's health. Fewer people suffered disease on high ground. The Greeks thought wet lowlands were less healthy. They were right. This was where mosquitoes were **breeding.** Mosquitos spread deadly **malaria.**

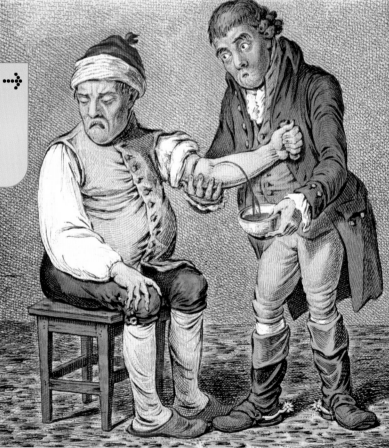

Word Bank   **bile**   fluid made by the liver to help digestion
hygiene   standards of cleanliness

Romans

The Romans knew that dirty water was unhealthy. They knew disease came with bad air, bad water, swamps, and **sewage.** In fact, they built public bathrooms so they could flush away all their sewage. Romans used to meet friends and sit and talk while all using the toilets at the same time!

Even though they had good **hygiene,** Romans often got **worms.** These were caught from poorly cooked or dirty food. They lived inside people's bodies.

Many Romans died from plagues. One plague lasted fifteen years. It killed up to 5,000 people a day in Rome alone.

Roman bathrooms got rid of waste and were popular meeting places!

Bad smell

"If soldiers are allowed to stay in one place too long, they are made miserable by the smell of their own excrement. The air becomes unhealthy and they catch diseases. **"**

Vegetius, a Roman writer from the 4th century

malaria   disease that causes fevers and chills. It is spread by mosquito bites.
phlegm   thick fluid in the lungs and throat

The Middle Ages

Oozing pus

"When scrofula develops, cut the swellings so that pus comes out. The scrofula should be scraped with a hook and drawn out."

Roger de Salerno, a doctor during the 1300s

The **Middle Ages** were a time of disease and **superstition.** There were all kinds of strange ideas about what caused disease and how it could be cured.

Beliefs

Many people believed that disease was a punishment. If you lived a bad life, you deserved to be sick. As a result, people often had no sympathy for the sick. Many doctors believed in magic and lucky charms to cure illness. A few herbs or spells might be the best help you could expect.

Urine samples are still tested for diseases.

Scrofula was a disease that often affected victims' necks in the Middle Ages.

Word Bank   **Middle Ages**   period of history roughly between
AD 500 and AD 1500

Finding a cure

Many **monks** grew and sold herbs as drugs. Local witches also used all kinds of plants to treat disease. They were probably just as good as the doctors of the period at curing illness!

One cure for **boils** used by doctors was to rub on herbs mixed with pig **dung**.

> "This will cure boils and the **pus** will disappear."
>
> From a 13th-century medical book

Many doctors looked at the color of a patient's **urine** to see what it showed about the patient. Today, doctors still look at urine samples—but the science is a little more advanced now!

Living to the old age of 100 was unheard of in the Middle Ages.

superstition belief based on magic or chance
urine liquid passed from the body, usually pale yellow

The Black Death

The 1300s were a terrible time for disease all over the world. People lived in fear that they would be the next to be struck by the dreaded **plague.** The disease became known as the Black Death because people's skin often turned dark purple.

People had no idea that **bacteria** in fleas spread the disease. Fleas drank the blood of diseased rats and then hopped onto people, cats, and dogs. When the fleas bit, the disease passed into the wound. Deadly bacteria soon got into the victim's bloodstream.

Killer disease

About 1330 a deadly plague began in China. Once people became sick, they **infected** others very quickly by sneezing. By 1350 travelers visiting China had taken the plague to most of Europe, where it killed 65 million people.

This painting from the Middle Ages shows victims of the bubonic plague.

Word Bank

buboes   swollen areas in the groin and armpits
fever   very high body temperature caused by illness

Lumps and blood

Victims of the Black Death got headaches, aching joints, **fever,** and **vomiting.** It took between one and seven days for **glands** to become swollen and painful. The glands were called **buboes,** which led to the name bubonic plague.

The Italian writer Boccaccio wrote:

> It began with swellings in the groin and armpit. Some of these were as big as apples and some were shaped like eggs.

Some other types of plague were spread by sneezes or even on people's clothes. These victims dribbled slimy **saliva** full of blood from their mouths and noses.

Pesky pigs

Two pigs pressed their snouts into the rags of a man who had just died from the plague. The pigs picked up the rags with their teeth and shook them. Within a short time, they both began to shake and fell dead on the ground.

Italian writer Boccaccio (1313–1375)

Fleas on rats carried the dreaded plague.

glands   parts of the body that make different chemicals
saliva   spit and fluid inside the mouth

Old and new worlds

The **Middle Ages** were a time of exploration. Sailors set out to find new lands. They brought back new treasures—but also new **bacteria** and disease. The sailors spread these diseases to people on different islands. The islanders died quickly, even from common colds, because they had no **immunity.**

In 1492 the explorer Christopher Columbus was the first European to sail his ship to an island in the Bahamas. He called it San Salvador. The **Native Americans** there began to die in the hundreds. Measles, **smallpox,** and flu quickly spread among them.

Sick sailors

Sailors began to travel the world in the Middle Ages. But a sailor's life was not very healthy. It was not just seasickness that caused their misery. Sailors often became sick for other reasons. Insect bites, bad food, and bacteria made life on a ship deadly.

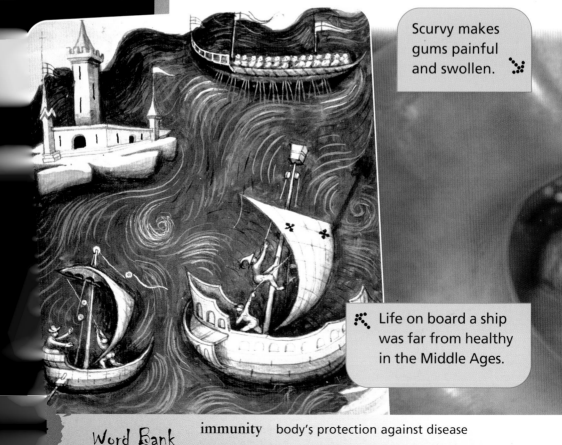

Scurvy makes gums painful and swollen.

Life on board a ship was far from healthy in the Middle Ages.

Word Bank   immunity   body's protection against disease

Bad food

Not all diseases were spread by bacteria. Food could also lead to terrible illness. Sailors out at sea for months on end often ate a poor diet of ship's biscuits, usually full of maggots.

A poor diet could cause a disease called **scurvy.** A person with scurvy could see his skin turn black with **ulcers,** his teeth fall out, and his gums rot. Victims often went crazy and died. But their misery could easily have been cured if they had eaten fruit. Scurvy was caused by a lack of **vitamin** C.

British sailors learned to take lime juice on their ships to prevent scurvy. They got the nickname "Limeys" because of this.

Scurvy

Vasco da Gama was a famous sailor from Portugal. Sixty-five percent of his crew died of scurvy while sailing to India in 1499.

Magellan was another sailor from Portugal. About 50 percent of his sailors died while crossing the Pacific Ocean.

scurvy   killer disease causing swollen, bleeding gums. It is caused by a lack of vitamin C.

Epidemic

A doctor's protection against the plague would have been useless against fleas!

The great plague

Doctors were at great risk during the plague. They wore leather gowns that were meant to protect them. In order to keep out smells, the outfit's beaklike nose was filled with herbs while the eyeholes were covered with glass. But it was not smells that spread the plague!

Each century has had a major **epidemic**. Nothing can stop some diseases from taking hold and spreading out of control.

The 1600s

The 1660s were not a good time for London. In 1665 bubonic **plague** killed up to 7,000 people a week. Within a few months, 55,000 people had died. That was about 20 percent of the total population of London.

Many people left the city for the countryside, where they hoped they would be safer. But they took the disease with them, and it spread even more.

Word Bank · **epidemic** outbreak of a disease that spreads quickly over a wide area

On the move

In 1665 a delivery of cloth was sent a long way from London to the village of Eyam, England. The man who received it died four days later. **Infected** fleas arrived on the cloth and brought the plague with them. After a few weeks, only about half of the 350 villagers were still alive.

In 1666 the plague was still spreading through London. Then, a huge fire swept through the city. It burned down 13,000 houses in four days. The flames also killed thousands of rats and their fleas. The fire stopped the plague at last.

Graveyard

Skeletons of plague victims have been found in London. **Mass graves** from 1665 show that bodies had been buried in a hurry, all piled in at once.

The great fire of London destroyed much of the city, including diseases.

mass graves huge graves where lots of people were buried together

Yellow fever

Yellow fever was another disease that spread on ships across the world. Mosquitoes bit sailors and gave them the deadly **virus.** When ships sailed on to new lands, other mosquitoes bit the **infected** sailors. These mosquitoes then carried the virus to more humans, and so the disease spread.

In 1793 a yellow fever **epidemic** hit Philadelphia. It killed roughly 4,000 people. For the next 30 years, yellow fever was one of the most feared diseases in U.S. cities where ships stopped.

Blood thirsty

Mosquitoes drink blood. When they stab the skin to feed, they can pass viruses into the victim's blood. That is how yellow fever spreads.

Yellow fever causes bleeding in the stomach. This blood then turns black as it is digested by juices in the stomach.

Yellow fever is spread by mosquitoes.

18

Word Bank

vaccine   medication to make the body defend itself against a disease

Black vomit

Yellow fever was also called yellow death because it caused liver damage. This turned the skin bright yellow.

It had other nasty effects, too. When a girl died of the disease in Memphis, Tennessee, in 1897, her uncle said that her screams could be heard down the street:

"Her tongue and lips were dark and cracked, and blood oozed from her mouth and nose. The most terrible thing was the black **vomit.** *It was as black as ink."*

Being protected against yellow fever in India.

The dreaded black vomit was a sign of yellow fever.

Vaccine at last

Scientists in New York developed a **vaccine** for yellow fever in the 1930s. Because of this vaccine, yellow fever is no longer the epidemic killer it once was. A single dose of the vaccine protects someone for at least ten years.

yellow fever   disease spread by mosquitoes, causing fever, aching limbs, and yellow skin

Measles is still common in poorer countries. There are about 40 million cases each year, with more than a million deaths. **Vaccines** for measles were first used in the 1960s, but poor countries cannot afford these expensive drugs.

Measles

Measles is a **virus** that can be spread by sneezing. You can also catch measles by sharing cups or spoons. Measles causes a rash, cough, and **fever**. It can be deadly.

The 1800s

- In 1846 a measles **epidemic** affected nearly 80 percent of people living on the Faeroe Islands, near Iceland.
- During the U.S. Civil War (from 1861 to 1865), there were nearly 100,000 cases of measles among four million soldiers. Almost 3,000 died.
- In 1875 British sailors took measles to Fiji by mistake. Nearly 40,000 islanders died.

A measles rash can be very itchy.

Word Bank   **antibiotic**   substance that kills harmful bacteria

Leprosy

Leprosy is often thought to affect poor people living in dirty places. In fact, it can affect anyone. Sores and **tumors** can destroy the face, often resulting in blindness. Leprosy also causes areas all over the body to go numb. It can spread through coughing and sneezing.

In 1995 there were about 1.8 million cases of leprosy in the world. Most of these were in Southeast Asia, Africa, and South America.

Some people in South America, Africa, and Southeast Asia still suffer from leprosy.

0   3000   6000 Miles

0   6000 Kilometres

Arctic Ocean

Asia

North America

Europe

Atlantic Ocean

Africa

Pacific Ocean

Pacific Ocean

South America

Indian Ocean

Oceania

N

Antarctica

Today, leprosy can be cured, as long as people can afford the right drugs.

tumor   unusual growth in the body

Flu

Flu **epidemics** do not just kill the old and weak. They can kill healthy people, too.

The 1900s

Less than 100 years ago, a major flu **pandemic** struck. It killed millions of people across the world.

In 1918, at the end of World War I, many people were on the move. A deadly type of flu was on the move as well. This flu killed young, healthy people. Half its victims were between the ages of 20 and 40.

By the end of 1918, twenty million people had died of the flu. In the United States, 550,000 people died in ten months.

Many children died from the flu in the 1800s.

Word Bank   **electron microscope**   microscope using electron beams to make images much larger

Fighting back

In 1918 microscopes were still unable to show the tiny flu **virus.** It was not until the 1930s that scientists developed new **electron microscopes.** At last, they could see and photograph flu viruses. This was a big step toward finding out about different kinds of the disease. Better **vaccines** were made to fight them. But viruses can change.

Even today, scientists have to be alert for new types of flu. They must be quick to send out new vaccines to stop another flu epidemic.

Police in Seattle, Washington, wore masks to guard them from flu.

The flu virus can be seen under a special microscope. ⋯

United States

In October 1918 195,000 Americans died from the flu.
- In New York, 851 people died in a single day.
- In Philadelphia, the city's death rate for one single week was 700 times higher than normal.

infected   carrying a disease-causing substance
pandemic   disease that spreads quickly across the world

Secrets in the Water

We need to drink water every day. But for many people, the water they need to live may also bring death. People always thought that if the water they drank looked clean, it was safe. They were wrong.

Causing a stink

In London in the 1850s, about 250 tons (227 tonnes) of human **excrement** flowed into the River Thames each day. The river was also used for drinking water!

In 1858 the summer was very hot, and water levels dropped. The river became known as the Great Stink. London was a **breeding** ground for disease.

Dung

Horses were once used everywhere. By 1900, 10 million tons (9 million tonnes) of horse dung was cleared from English towns each year. This was a breeding site for flies and rats.

Human excrement was put into cesspits. But these seeped into the soil and **wells,** so drinking water became **polluted.**

Maxwell Street was once a **slum** area in Chicago.

Word Bank

cesspit   hole dug to hold waste and sewage
excrement   body waste

Chicago

In the 1800s no one realized the link between **sewage** and disease. People in Chicago, Illinois, used the river for water and as a waste dump. Animals were kept in alleys, and their **dung** was dumped into Chicago's streets. Rainwater washed this into the river and **cesspits.** This mixture would seep into the water supply.

Diseases such as **typhoid** and **cholera** spread quickly. It was not until big pipes were built to carry waste away that Chicago finally became clean and safe.

Animal waste

More than two million cows, sheep, and pigs were brought to London markets in 1876. In some parts of London, there were far more pigs than people. That was a lot of manure to clog the streets and drain into the water supply!

Chicago needed huge sewer pipes to make the city clean and safe.

pollute   make air or water dirty or unsafe
well   hole dug down into the ground for getting water

Typhoid

Typhoid is deadly. It begins like the flu and, in a week, a red rash appears on the chest and back. Then comes **diarrhea** and a dry mouth. The disease can kill in a few weeks.

During the 1800s, many doctors thought typhoid was carried in the bad smells of dirty cities. They did not know that the dirty water was actually the problem.

Chicago had more typhoid deaths in the 1880s than any other city in the world. It was at this time that the scientist Carl Eberth discovered the **bacteria** that caused the disease. The cure came many years later.

Mary Mallon was locked up in an institution until she died in 1938.

Word Bank   **diarrhea**   frequent loose or watery waste

Dangerous lady

In 1906 there were 3,467 cases of typhoid in New York, with 639 deaths. The most famous typhoid carrier was Mary Mallon.

"Typhoid Mary" was hired as a cook in a New York house in the early 1900s. Within weeks, six people in the house caught typhoid. Doctors gave Mary tests. They found she was carrying the disease, but she was not affected herself. She was told to keep away from kitchens.

Twenty people caught typhoid at a New York hospital in 1915. The police found that the cook was Mary Mallon, and they took her away to be locked up.

Did you know?

Typhoid was not just the disease of dirty city streets. The drains of Windsor Castle, where English royalty lived, also carried typhoid bacteria. Prince Albert, the husband of Queen Victoria, died in 1861 from typhoid fever.

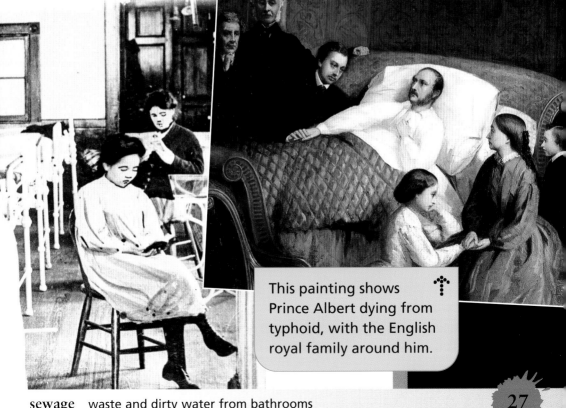

This painting shows Prince Albert dying from typhoid, with the English royal family around him.

sewage   waste and dirty water from bathrooms

Cholera

Cholera is a disease that attacks the **intestines**. Victims have severe **diarrhea** and **vomiting**. Today, cholera can be cured if treated quickly. This means getting fluid and salts back into the body quickly. Then, a course of **antibiotics** can kill the **bacteria.**

Doctor John Snow, who discovered that cholera was carried in dirty water.

In the past, doctors could do little about cholera. In 1854 it killed 6 percent of the people of Chicago. About 60 people died of the disease each day. The city's streets were lined with coffins.

Recent cholera epidemics

- **1971:** Bangladesh, Asia, 6,500 deaths.
- **1991:** Peru, South America, 3,000 deaths.
- **1994:** Rwanda, Africa, 20,000 deaths.

The disease spreads when drinking water becomes **polluted** by sewers. Many poor countries do not have clean water supplies. Cholera still exists in these countries.

A cartoon from 1858 shows Father Thames bringing **diphtheria,** cholera, and **scrofula** to children in London.

Word Bank   **intestine**   part of the body that goes from the stomach to the anus. It is where food is digested.

Discovery

In 1832 cholera spread through Europe and the United States. In Paris 7,000 people died in a few months.

A British doctor, John Snow, was sure cholera was caught from water. But he could not convince other doctors about this. Everyone thought cholera spread in smelly air.

Ideas changed after a mother washed her baby's diaper in a London **well** in 1854. A cholera **epidemic** began.

John Snow proved that the 616 victims who died all drank from the same well. His work led to the discovery of cholera bacteria 30 years later.

Imagine that!

German scientist Max von Pettenkofer was not so sure that cholera was caught from drinking water. To try to prove this, he put live cholera bacteria into water and drank it. He soon got an upset stomach, but survived his unwise test.

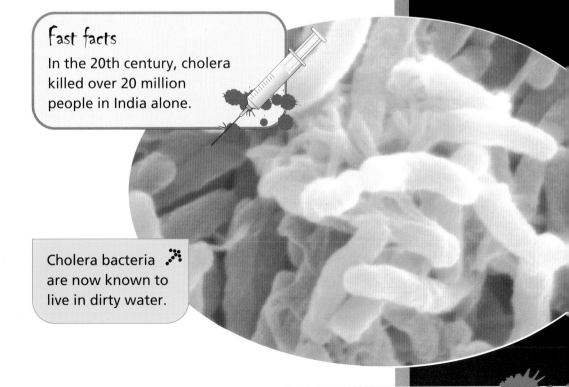

Fast facts
In the 20th century, cholera killed over 20 million people in India alone.

Cholera bacteria are now known to live in dirty water.

diptheria   disease that causes a high fever and makes your throat so swollen that breathing is difficult

Polio is a very **infectious** disease. It causes **fever,** headache, **vomiting,** stiffness in the neck, and painful limbs. Polio can cause **paralysis** or even lead to death by **suffocation.** The only way to prevent it is with a vaccine.

Polio

Polio is a **virus** that damages the **nervous system.** It has killed and disabled people throughout history.

Children often caught polio at swimming pools or from **infected** drinking water. Many victims died from being unable to breathe. Other victims lost the use of their legs. They could only walk with crutches. **Epidemics** all around the world were common until **vaccines** were discovered.

Fast facts

In 1928 a machine called an iron lung was invented. Polio sufferers had to lie inside it while a pump helped them to breathe.

Children with polio needed special supports to straighten their legs.

Word Bank
nervous system   how messages are sent around the body from the brain

War

Franklin Roosevelt was president of the United States in the 1930s. He caught polio when he was a child. Roosevelt called for a "war on polio" and did a lot to help research into the disease.

In the 1940s scientists Jonas Salk and Albert Sabin worked on monkeys to develop a vaccine for polio. In 1955 they were successful. Their work has saved the lives of millions of children. The United States became polio-free in 1979.

Happy ending

Great efforts have been made to stamp out polio once and for all. In 2001, 575 million children were vaccinated in 94 countries. That year, fewer than 500 polio cases were reported worldwide.

Polio patients were helped to breathe with iron lungs.

paralysis unable to move
suffocation unable to breathe

Great Discoveries

Some people have made a huge difference in the fight against disease. Key events have led to important discoveries.

Smallpox

Smallpox was a terrible disease. It caused the skin to bubble up in nasty blisters. Victims usually died from **fever.** Smallpox was spread through direct contact with an **infected** person or with their clothes or bedding. In the 1700s, smallpox killed a third of those who caught it.

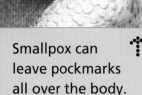

Smallpox can leave pockmarks all over the body.

Europeans who moved to the United States took smallpox with them. The disease spread and killed many **Native Americans.**

Easily spread

Smallpox was feared in the 1700s. People had the disease for about twelve days before they felt sick. They infected others without knowing. Those who survived were often left blind and scarred by deep **pockmarks.**

Fast facts

Vaccinate comes from the Latin word *vacca*, meaning "cow."

A cartoon from 1802 made fun of vaccination by showing that it turned patients into cows!

Word Bank **pockmark** round scar left on the skin after a pox disease

Edward Jenner

Edward Jenner was an English doctor born in the 1700s. He noticed that women working in dairies never caught smallpox. Instead, they got a weak form of smallpox called cowpox.

The women got blisters on their hands from milking cows that carried the disease. Jenner thought the **pus** in these blisters protected them from catching smallpox.

He **injected** pus from cowpox blisters into a **volunteer** named James. Then, Jenner injected him with smallpox. James became sick, but in a few days he made an amazing recovery. Jenner had found out how to vaccinate people against the dreaded smallpox.

Doctor Edward Jenner.

Wiped out

- Smallpox killed between 300 and 500 million people in the 1900s.
- In the 1970s, worldwide vaccination was carried out.
- In 1980 smallpox was wiped out at last.

volunteer   someone who offers to take part in something

Louis Pasteur

French scientist Louis Pasteur (below) first developed the idea that tiny living things could get into our bodies and attack us. He found that these "**bacteria**" could live in soil, water, air, plants, and animals. Pasteur believed that some bacteria caused disease. He set about proving his ideas to other scientists.

Fast facts

We have Louis Pasteur to thank for our cartons of bacteria-free milk today. Pasteurised milk is heated to make it safe to drink.

Louis Pasteur poses for a photograph.

Anthrax

Anthrax is a deadly animal disease that can pass to humans in wool, cloth, and leather. Pasteur began working with anthrax bacteria. He was sure bacteria could cause disease and wanted to find ways of killing bacteria in the body.

Pasteur discovered that one kind of bacteria could attack and kill another kind. He tried this with anthrax and developed a **vaccine** for the disease.

Success!

In 1882 Pasteur tested his anthrax vaccine on sheep. He gave his vaccine to one group but not the other. All the sheep were then **injected** with anthrax bacteria. The sheep that had the vaccine were fine, while all the others died. Pasteur's ideas were right!

Sheep being vaccinated against anthrax in New Guinea in 1925.

Rabies

Rabies is a deadly **virus.** People catch it by being bitten by an **infected** animal. The disease starts with **fever,** headache, and pain around the bitten area. It leads to **spasms,** a fear of water, madness, **coma,** and death.

Louis Pasteur and his team knew that rabies attacked the **nervous system** and the brain. By taking **cells** from **spinal cords** of dead victims, he made a **vaccine.** It seemed to work on animals. But would it do the same for humans?

Pasteur and his team take saliva from a dog with rabies.

Danger

Dogs with rabies are very dangerous. Louis Pasteur needed help with his experiments to find a rabies vaccine. Members of his team had to hold down a dog while he tried to collect the **saliva.** Pasteur then studied the virus in the saliva.

This dog has rabies.

Word Bank

cells   tiny building blocks that make up all living things
coma   deep sleeplike state caused by injury or disease

Risk

In 1885 a dog with rabies bit a boy named Joseph. He would have died in agony if nothing were done, so he was taken to Louis Pasteur, who decided to try out his vaccine. It was a risk, but Joseph survived and was soon well again. Pasteur now knew that his rabies vaccine worked.

The following year, about 2,500 people were treated for rabies. When Pasteur died in 1895, 20,000 people had been successfully treated.

Did you know?

- Rabies is found all over the world, except for Australia, Antarctica, and some small islands.
- In the United States, about one person every year dies from rabies.
- Worldwide, between 45,000 and 60,000 people die each year from rabies. They do not get the vaccine in time.

spasm   sudden, uncontrolled movement of muscles
spinal cord   bundle of nerves that runs down the backbone

During the 1700s and 1800s, TB killed millions of people. It was the main cause of death in Europe and the United States. Another name for the disease was consumption.

Deadly lung disease

Tuberculosis (or TB) was a disease everyone feared well into the 1900s. It was a serious disease of the lungs. Coughing and sneezing meant it spread quickly in crowded **slums.**

Doctors thought TB patients needed fresh air. They often moved their beds outside—even in the snow! This did little to make patients feel better. They already had a bad cough, tiredness, no appetite, and a **fever**. They often coughed up blood, too. TB was a miserable killer disease.

Patients were put outside at this TB hospital in Nottingham, England, in 1933. The fresh air was thought to be good for them.

Word Bank

infectious   spreads easily from one person to another
Nobel Prize   international prize awarded for important work

Robert Koch

In 1882 the German doctor Robert Koch found the **bacteria** that caused TB. He and his team had searched for a long time, and it was a great breakthrough. The following year, he found the bacteria that caused **cholera.** Only then could scientists get to work on making **vaccines** for the diseases.

Robert Koch's work helped fight diseases that still killed millions of people into the 1900s. In 1891 he set up a center for **infectious** diseases in Berlin, Germany. In 1905 Robert Koch received the famous **Nobel Prize** for his lifesaving work.

TB today

Even today in the 21st century, TB kills over one million people each year. Those who live in poor, damp, and crowded places can still become **infected.**

Doctor Robert Koch working in his science lab.

slums   poor, dirty housing in overcrowded parts of a city
tuberculosis   disease that causes fever and lung failure

During World War I, doctors cleaned soldiers' wounds with **antiseptic.** Alexander Fleming found that this often killed white **cells** in the patients' blood. These cells are important in fighting infection. The good cells were being destroyed faster than the harmful bacteria.

Penicillin

A great discovery in the last 100 years was a type of drug called an **antibiotic.** It changed the fight against disease forever. The drug was made from **mold.** Some mold can kill harmful **bacteria.**

The world's first antibiotic was called penicillin. Doctors began using it in the 1940s. Since then, it has saved millions of lives by fighting **infection.** The number of children dying from **pneumonia** has fallen by 93 percent due to penicillin.

Alexander Fleming ⋯⁖ at work in his laboratory in France in 1916.

Word Bank

antiseptic   substance that stops harmful bacteria from growing and spreading disease

Alexander Fleming

In 1928 Alexander Fleming made history. He came back from vacation to his lab in London and found that mold had grown on a dish of pneumonia bacteria. Fleming was amazed to find the mold had killed the bacteria. This mold was called penicillin.

Soon other scientists got to work on Fleming's discovery. Howard Florey was an Australian scientist working in the United Kingdom. In 1940 he and his team found that penicillin was good at fighting all kinds of disease. Florey's team grew the mold in milk churns, lemonade bottles, and bedpans. Then, they tried it on a patient. It worked!

Mold began to grow over Fleming's dish.

Mold

Alexander Fleming made his discovery by mistake! It was all because he left the lid off of a bacteria-coated dish when he went on vacation. Thank goodness he did!

mold   type of fungus that grows in damp places
pneumonia   disease of the lungs that makes it difficult to breathe

Up to Date

Each year we understand more about disease. We have made amazing progress in the last 30 years. But there is still plenty to learn.

AIDS

During the late 1970s, doctors in New York and California reported many cases of a rare kind of cancer and **pneumonia** in young men. These diseases were taking hold because the men's **immune systems** were failing. They seemed unable to fight **infections.** A new **virus** made them sick.

In the early 1980s, the new condition caused by this Human Immunodeficiency Virus (HIV) was named AIDS. This stands for Acquired Immune Deficiency Syndrome.

Did you know?

- More than 90 percent of people with AIDS live in poor countries where sex education is often not available.
- Every minute, five people between the ages of 10 and 24 are infected with HIV somewhere in the world.

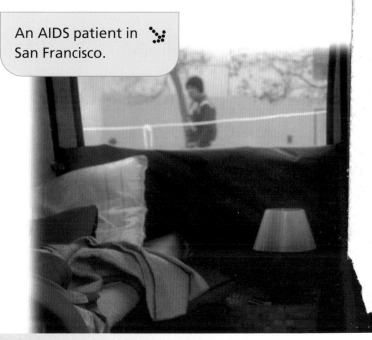

An AIDS patient in San Francisco.

Word Bank

immune system   body's way of defending against disease
orphan   someone, especially a child, whose parents are dead

HIV

Many people (male and female) today carry the HIV virus. It does not always develop into AIDS. Unlike other viruses, HIV is not passed by sneezing or touching. You can only be **infected** through exchanging body fluids such as blood or **semen.**

If the virus develops into AIDS, the patient's immune system fails to fight infections properly. There is still no cure for the disease. More than 20 million people have died of AIDS. The number of people living with the HIV virus is now about 42 million.

Many African children are orphaned after AIDS has killed their parents.

semen   bodily fluid that contains sperm

Parasites

Many tiny creatures live in or on the human body. Even clean human skin contains about five million **bacteria** per square centimeter.

At least 80 different kinds of bacteria live in the human mouth without causing harm. But larger **parasites** are killers in some parts of the world.

Some types of **worm** get inside humans through uncooked food. Tapeworms can grow up to 33 feet (10 meters) long inside people! Round worms are caught from **infected** water or food. These worms infect a billion people worldwide. They kill 20,000 people a year by blocking up their **intestines.**

Just one bite

One type of mosquito spreads a worm that does real damage to people. When it bites, the female mosquito **injects** tiny worm **larvae** into the bloodstream. The worm grows and causes a disease called **elephantiasis** that makes the legs swell up.

Elephantiasis can make walking very difficult.

Some tapeworms grow to 33 feet (10 meters) long!

Word Bank   **elephantiasis**   huge swelling of an arm or a leg caused by a type of worm

Malaria

Mosquitoes can be deadly. If an infected mosquito bites someone, it passes a **virus** into the blood. **Malaria** is a flulike illness that lasts between ten and twenty days. If it affects the kidneys or brain, it can kill.

In the last 2,000 years, malaria may have caused half of all human deaths on the planet. Today, many people survive malaria with modern drugs. Even so, it kills over one million people each year. In fact, more people die from malaria today than they did 30 years ago.

The deadly *Anopheles* mosquito spreads malaria.

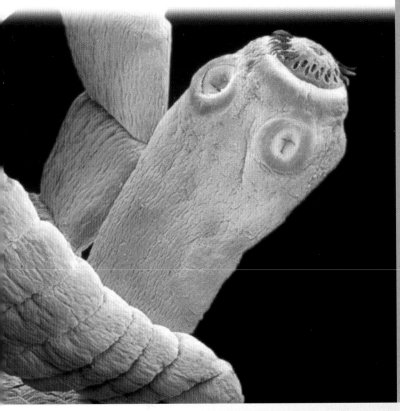

Did you know?

- Malaria now infects 300 million people each year. The young and old are at most risk of dying.
- Two children die of malaria every minute.
- Ninety percent of all malaria cases are in Africa, where it is the main cause of death in the 21st century.

parasite   living thing that lives or feeds on other living things, often harming them

Cancer news

One of the most feared diseases of modern times is cancer. It is feared because more people seem to develop it now. That is because we survive other diseases and live longer.

Cancer develops when **cells** begin to grow out of control inside the body. Although there are many kinds of cancer, they all start because of abnormal (not normal) cells.

Cancer cells often form a **tumor.** Tumors can grow in most parts of the body. Some cancers, such as **leukemia,** affect the blood. Cancer cells often travel to other parts of the body, where they can grow and take over normal cells. This is how cancer spreads through the body.

Cancer researchers test anticancer drugs.

Word Bank   leukemia   type of cancer that affects the blood cells

Progress

A third of people in wealthier countries get cancer at some time in their lives. One fifth of these die of the disease. Scientists are working hard to find out how cells develop cancer. By finding what causes this, they hope to make new anticancer drugs.

Doctors are making great progress in treating the disease. When cancer is caught early, doctors today are often able to stop the cells from growing. The good news is that in the last ten years, the death rate from cancer has fallen by 12 percent.

The dark area on this liver is a tumor caused by cancer.

Giant tumor

In 1999 Marie Bell, seventeen, had stomach pains. She went to a hospital in Maryland, where doctors found a 79-pound (36-kilogram) tumor the size of a beach ball in her ovary (the organ that makes eggs). Four doctors removed it in a four-hour operation.

Bird flu

Many diseases are no longer the problem they once were. The bad news is, some of the old diseases can **adapt.** New types of flu can suddenly break out. With modern air travel, a new **virus** can cross the world in a few hours.

We can still catch a few diseases from animals. Birds catch a type of flu and pass it on to humans. In 2004 people were worried about a new flu **epidemic** spread by birds. Bird flu started in Vietnam. The virus spread through hens in Asia. Eleven people died after catching the disease.

Super bugs

Antibiotics have saved many lives—but there is a problem. Each time a patient takes an antibiotic for an **infection,** the drug may not kill all the **bacteria.** A few may survive and adapt in order to beat the drug. These can **breed** to make super bugs that antibiotics cannot kill.

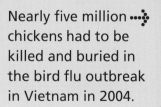

Nearly five million ⋯⋗ chickens had to be killed and buried in the bird flu outbreak in Vietnam in 2004.

Word Bank   **adapt**   alter to fit in with new conditions by becoming slightly different

SARS

A new disease broke out in China in 2002. It was called SARS, which stands for Severe Acute **Respiratory** Syndrome. People worried that it might become a serious epidemic. In fact, only 8,098 people caught SARS worldwide. Of these, 774 died.

People in Japan, China, and Hong Kong wore medical masks in the streets. They were scared they would breathe in the new virus. In Ontario, Canada, there was a big SARS scare. People were not allowed to travel for a while. This was to stop the disease from spreading.

Mad cow disease

A new brain disease affected cows in the 1990s. Some people then developed a similar disease. They had probably eaten **infected** beef. This human form of the disease is called new variant CJD. Between 1996 and 2002, 129 people developed new variant CJD in the United Kingdom. There is no cure yet, and infected people will die.

People wear masks in a street in Hong Kong to protect them from SARS.

Latest developments

All around the world, scientists are looking into different diseases. They are trying to find answers to health problems that have troubled humans for years.

There are signs of progress in fighting a **virus** that affects people in parts of Africa. A disease called **ebola,** which causes bleeding inside the body, kills over 75 percent of its victims. At the moment there is no cure for this disease. But in 2004, scientists working on mice reported big steps that could lead to a safe human **vaccine** in the future.

Old and healthy

We are all living longer today than ever before. One disease that still affects older people today is called Alzheimer's. This is when the brain no longer works properly. But already scientists are developing new drugs that may help to keep Alzheimer's under control.

Many older people today keep healthy and active.

Word Bank   digest   break food down into little bits

Breakthrough

A team of British scientists has been working on a vaccine for some types of cancer. An important step in 2004 was developing a vaccine against **leukemia**. Doctors tested the vaccine on mice with the disease and found the mice lived much longer as a result. It would be like humans having another 25 years of life.

The world awaits the next great discovery in the long war against disease. It is a fight that began thousands of years ago. The war is far from over, but many of the battles have already been won.

Healthy bacteria

Ninety-nine percent of all **bacteria** are useful. Bacteria help our bodies **digest** food and make important **vitamins.** There are more bacteria in your body than there are people on the planet!

Scientists keep making new discoveries to fight disease.

ebola   disease causing quick death through massive blood loss
vitamin   substance needed in food to keep us healthy

Find Out More

Did you know?

- **Leprosy** is the oldest known disease in the world. Cases of this nasty disease were first described in ancient Egypt as early as 1350 BC.

- There are 180 different types of the **virus** that causes the world's most **infectious** disease: the common cold.

Books

Parker, Steve. *Groundbreakers: Alexander Fleming.* Chicago: Heinemann Library, 2001.

Sneddon, Robert. *Microlife: Fighting Infectious Diseases.* Chicago: Heinemann Library, 2000.

Woolf, Alex. *Death and Disease.* Farmington Hills, MI: Gale, 2004.

Using the Internet

Explore the Internet to find out more about medicine through the ages. You can use a search engine, such as www.yahooligans.com, and type in keywords such as:

- **plague**;
- **tuberculosis**;
- medicine + United States Civil War; and
- Louis Pasteur.

Search tips

There are billions of pages on the Internet, so it can be difficult to find exactly what you are looking for.

These search tips will help you find useful websites more quickly:

- Know exactly what you want to find out about first.
- Use two to six keywords in a search, putting the most important words first.
- Be precise. Only use names of people, places, or things.

Glossary

adapt   alter to fit in with new conditions by becoming slightly different

antibiotic   substance that kills harmful bacteria

antiseptic   substance that stops harmful bacteria from growing and spreading disease

bacteria   group of tiny living things. Some can cause disease.

bile   fluid made by the liver to help digestion

boil   swollen infection on the skin that is red and sore

bowel   part of the intestine where waste is held before being let out of the body

breeding   process of creating offspring or more of something

buboes   swollen areas in the groin and armpits

cells   tiny building blocks that make up all living things

cesspit   hole dug to hold waste and sewage

cholera   disease causing severe stomachaches, which can kill

coma   deep sleeplike state caused by injury or disease

diarrhea   frequent loose or watery waste

digest   break food down into little bits

diptheria   disease that causes a high fever and makes your throat so swollen that breathing is difficult

dung   waste matter (manure) from an animal

ebola   disease causing quick death through massive blood loss

electron microscope   microscope using electron beams to make images much larger

elephantiasis   huge swelling of an arm or a leg caused by a type of worm

epidemic   outbreak of a disease that spreads quickly over a wide area

excrement   body waste

fever   very high body temperature caused by illness

glands   parts of the body that make different chemicals

hygiene   standards of cleanliness

immune system   body's way of defending itself against disease

immunity   body's protection against disease

infected   carrying a disease-causing substance in your system. Also, to pass on such a substance.

infection   disease-causing substance that has taken hold in your body

infectious   spreads easily from one person to another

inject   to force a liquid into the body (for example, a shot)

intestine   part of the body that goes from the stomach to the anus. It is where food is digested.

larvae   immature form of an insect or worm

leprosy   disease that causes damage to the nerves and skin

leukemia   type of cancer that affects the blood cells

malaria   disease that causes fever and chills. It is spread by mosquito bites.

mass graves   huge graves where lots of people were buried together

Middle Ages   period of history roughly between AD 500 and AD 1500

monk   member of a religious community of men

mold   type of fungus that grows in damp places

Native American   member of any tribe of Indian in North America, South America, and the Arctic

nervous system   how messages are sent around the body from the brain

Nobel Prize   international prize awarded for important work

organism   living cell or group of cells

orphan   someone, especially a child, whose parents are dead

pandemic   disease that spreads quickly across the world

paralysis   unable to move

parasite   living thing that lives or feeds on other living things, often harming them

phlegm   thick fluid in the lungs and throat

plague   deadly disease that spreads quickly

pneumonia   disease of the lungs that makes it difficult to breathe

pockmark   round scar left on the skin after a pox disease

pollute   make air or water dirty or unsafe

pox   any disease that causes a rash of pus-filled sores

pus   thick yellow or greenish foul-smelling liquid made by infected wounds

respiratory   to do with breathing and the lungs

saliva spit and fluid inside the mouth

scrofula disease causing swellings, common in the Middle Ages

scurvy killer disease causing swollen, bleeding gums. It is caused by a lack of vitamin C.

semen bodily fluid that has sperm

senna powder made from the seeds of the cassia tree

sewage waste and dirty water from bathrooms

slums poor, dirty housing in overcrowded parts of a city

smallpox infectious disease causing blisters all over the body

spasm sudden, uncontrolled movement of muscles

spinal cord bundle of nerves that runs down the backbone

suffocation unable to breathe

superstition belief based on magic or chance

tribe group of people living closely together, sharing the same beliefs and customs

tuberculosis disease that causes fever and lung failure

tumor unusual growth in the body

typhoid disease spread by eating food or water with bacteria in it

ulcer open sore. It is often full of pus.

urine liquid passed from the body, usually pale yellow

vaccine medication to make the body defend itself against a disease

virus tiny living thing that breaks into the body's cells and can cause disease

vitamin substance needed in small amounts in our food to keep us healthy

volunteer someone who offers to take part in something

vomit throw up

well hole dug down into the ground for getting water

whooping cough disease causing coughing fits and breathing difficulties

worm kind of parasite that lives in the human body

yellow fever disease spread by mosquitoes, causing fever, aching limbs, and yellow skin

Index